The S

words by Jill McDougall
photographs by Lisa James

You need a bucket.

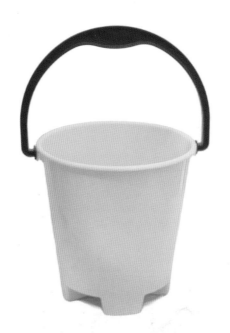

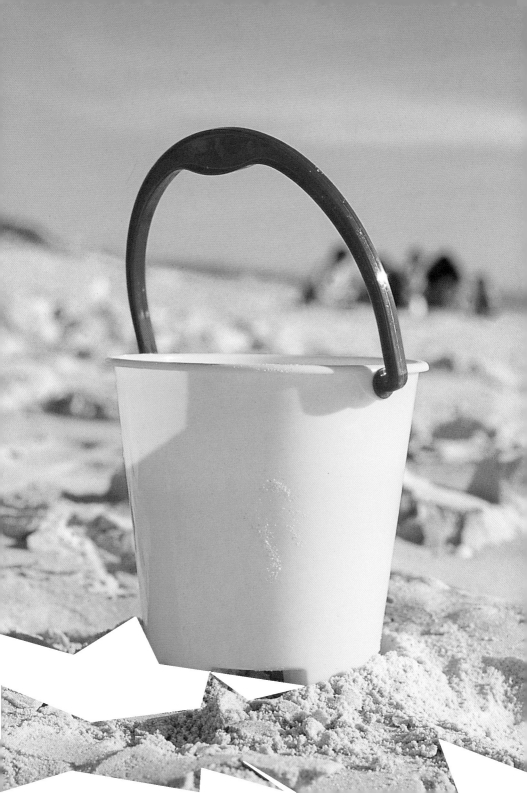

You need a spade.

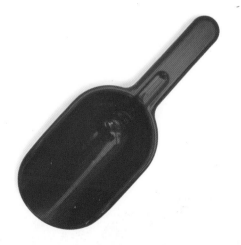

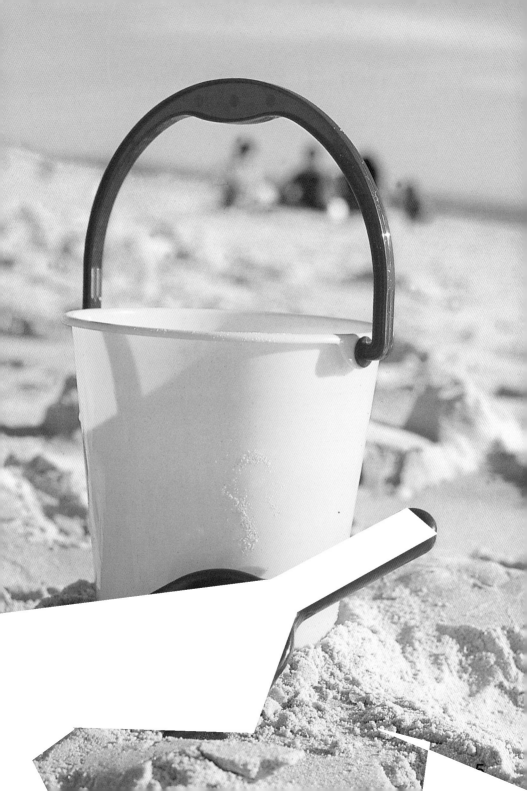

You need sand.

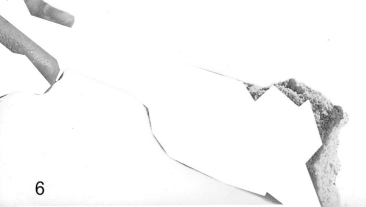

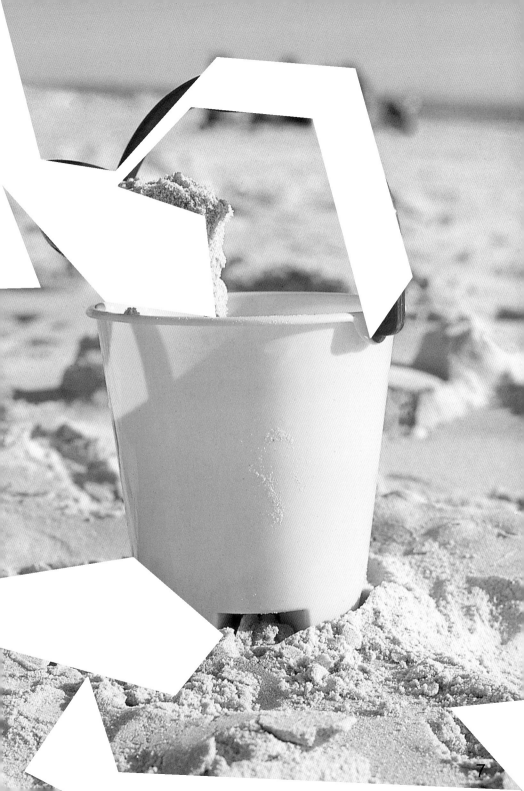

You need shells.

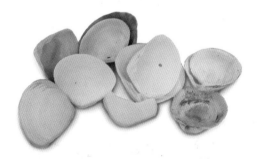

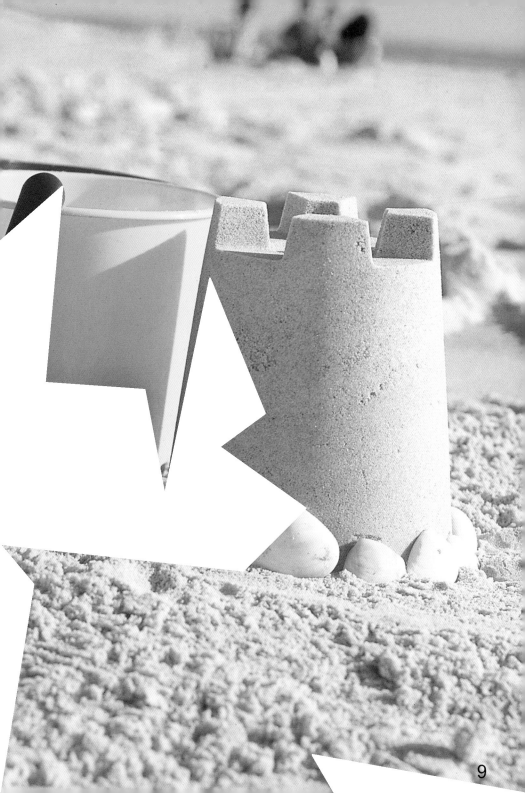

You need seaweed.

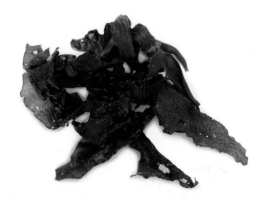

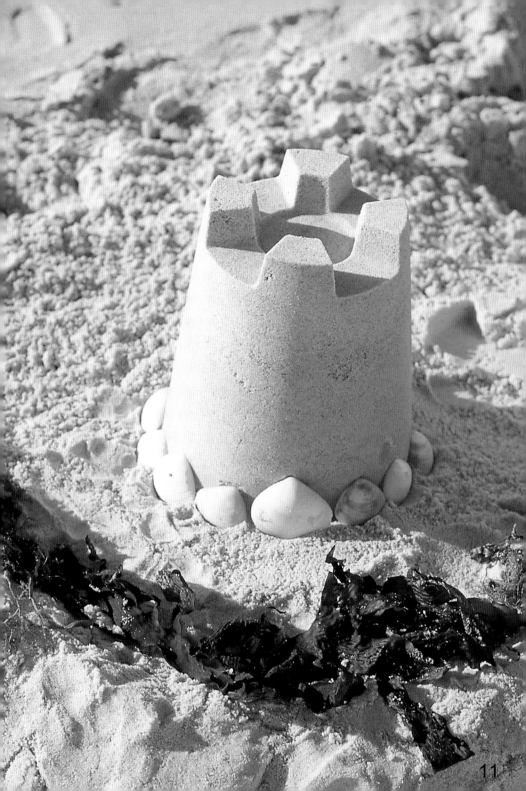

You need water.

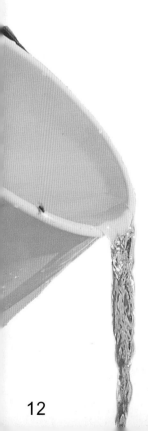

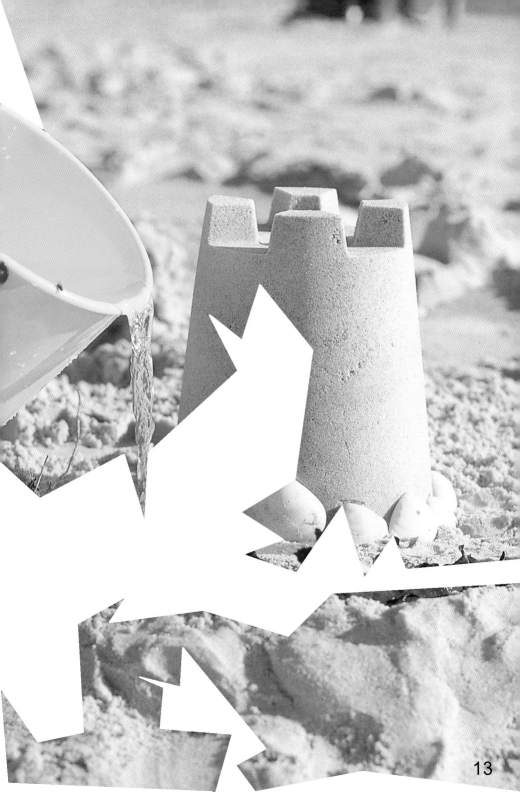

13

You need a leaf.

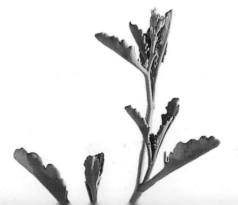

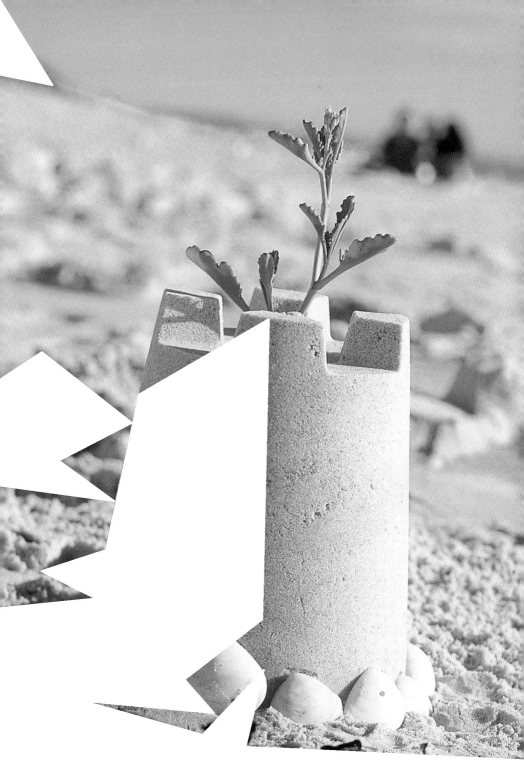

You do not need a wave!

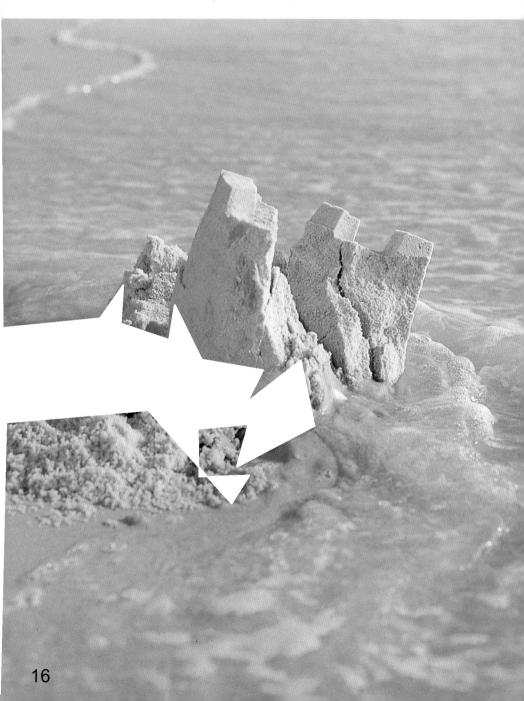